2,001 Things That Won't Make It Into the 21st Century

2,001 Things
That Won't
Make It
Into the
21st Century

compiled by Career Press

CAREER
PRESS
FRANKLIN
LAKES, NJ

2,001 THINGS THAT WON'T MAKE IT INTO THE 21ST CENTURY
Cover design by Lu Rossman
Printed in the U.S.A. by Book-mart Press

To order this title, please call toll-free 1-800-CAREER-1 (NJ and Canada: 201-848-0310) to order using VISA or MasterCard, or for further information on books from Career Press.

Library of Congress Cataloging-in-Publication Data

2001 things that won't make it into the 21st century / compiled by Career Press.
    p.   cm.
  ISBN 1-56414-439-9 (pbk.)
   1. United States—Civilization—20th century Miscellanea.
 2. Popular culture—United States—History—20th century Miscellanea. 3. Twenty-first century—Forecasts Miscellanea.
I. Career Press Inc. II. Title: Two thousand and one things that won't make it into the 21st century. III. Title: Two thousand one things that won't make it into the 21st century.
E16912.A18   1999
973.9—dc21   99-41526

Acknowledgments

Many thanks to the people who contributed their ideas, memories, and personal touches to the publication of this book:

The employees of Career Press; their families and friends; Career Press authors: Robert Bly, Laurie Borman, Theresa Foy DiGeronimo, Gary Greenberg, Riki Intner, Ken Lloyd, Loriann Oberlin, Mary Snyder, Charles Watson, Jim Yoakum; and literary agent Mike Snell.

...And to *all* contest participants, including the winner of our contest, John Bennett of Bennett Book Nook, Wyckoff, N.J., whose winning entry, "The doubleheader," can be found under "Sports."

Finally, a special thanks to Jackie Michaels of Career Press, who spearheaded this project and dedicated countless hours to filling its pages. Jackie inspired us all to delve into our past and relive some of our favorite memories. We thank her for her endless hard work and for giving us a reason to be nostalgic.

2001
2001
2001

Introduction (and disclaimer)

We hope this book is received in the lighthearted way in which it was written. It has been a collaboration of many efforts and is based purely on opinion, speculation, and conjecture. Our purpose in writing it is to provide a nostalgic glimpse at our lives as we enter a new millennium.

Now that we've jogged your memory, you can add your own ideas to our list. We were limited by space, but you are limited only by your own imagination.

Have fun—we certainly did!

2001

2001

2001

Life in the 20th century

2001 2001

2001

Fashion

Nehru jacket and shirt

Leisure suits

Indian love beads

Poodle skirts

Parachute pants

Oh the memories. Blue with rainbowed detailing. Oh, I miss those pants. If you too miss those old swooshy pairs of baggy nylon joy, don't fear! For only $88.50 per pair (plus shipping) you can order a new pair of parachute pants at parachute-pants.com.

Leg warmers

Toe socks

Cinch belts

Bangle bracelets

White gloves and hats ensemble for women

12

Tie tacks

Crinoline

Wigwams (baggy socks)

Turtleneck dickeys

Elevator shoes

Thin leather ties

Extra wide ties

Desert boots

Disco bags

Earthshoes

Vans

"Jazz" shoes

Members Only jacket

Ripped t-shirts

Thin metal slinky belts

Gauchos

Bell bottoms

Culottes

Knickers

Macrame bikini

String bikini

Macrame vest

What goes around, comes around. Except, who would have thought that one of the more outlandish pants styles of 60s hippiedom and free spiritness would blast through the hermetic clothing styles of the 90s? And then there's platform shoes...

Fashion

14

Anything gold lamé

Fringe vests

Belts with changeable colored bands

Designer jeans
- Vanderbilt
- JouJou
- Sassoon
- Jordache
- Corniche
- No Excuses
- Zipper cuff
- Guess
- Sergio Valente

The multilayered preppy look

Girdles

Big velvet bow ties

Alligator or snakeskin shoes

Fur coats

Boot jewelry

Le Sports sac handbags

Corsets

Garter belts

Stockings with seams

Penny loafers with pennies

Penny loafers without pennies

Big bows in hair or on a dress

Pop-it necklaces

Fashion

Bowling shirts with name stitched on pocket

Tube tops

Coonskin hats

Bubble skirts

Faux tuxedo T-shirts

Pixie shoes

Happy landings shoes

Baby doll pajamas

T-shirt ties

Capri pants

Stiletto heels

Thong underwear for men

Beatle boots

Bat-wing eyeglasses

Fruit loops on back of shirts

Letter sweaters

Tiki necklaces

Choker necklaces

Leather bracelets

Granny glasses

Mini-, midi-, and maxi-skirts

Shoe taps

Fashion

18

French cuffs

High-heeled sneakers

Friendship bracelets

Slips and petticoats

Crocheted knee-high socks

Saddle shoes

Peds

Zoot suits

Fedora

Medieval look

Empire dresses

Fashion

Peasant blouses

Shirt-tail dresses

Halter tops

Trouser cuffs

Epilets

Pocket flaps

Pleats

Wing-tip shoes

Black leather skintight pants and jackets

Pea coats

Pill box hats

Hip huggers

Pants worn below the waist

80s fashion

Swatch watches

Jeans with zipper at the ankle

Tough skins jeans

Benneton "B" sweaters

Jeannie pants

The *Miami Vice* look

Skids

Panama Jack clothing

Surfer gear

"Choose life" T-shirts

Anything florescent or tie-dyed

Wearing multiple pairs of colored socks

Z. Cavaricci jeans

Colored mascara

Suspenders

Stirrup pants

Friendship beads

JAMS shorts

Wearing your collar up

Fashion

Black Jellie bracelets

Coca-Cola brand clothing

Belts worn around sweater or long shirt

Black plastic rubber band bracelets

Anything on earrings

Black or silver lamé Porsche/Ferrari jackets

Hair trends

Setting hair with beer

Mutton chops

Banana clips

Epilady hair remover

Hair trends

Prell shampoo

Brylcreem

"A little dab'll do ya'!" Brylcreem was introduced in the 40s and 50s to the enjoyment of greasers and "Sha Na Na" cast members. One of the original "hair gels," Brylcreem has undergone a major drop in sales, but it's still on the market…for now.

Jheri Curls

Pin curls

Dippity Doo

Afro

Bouffant

Beehive hairdo

Stretch headband

Using beer cans to roll hair

Crimped hair

Mohawk

Ironing hair

Mall hair/high hair

Shag

Dorothy Hammill wedge

Bo Derek look

Farrah Fawcett look

Hair-in-a-can

Big bows at nape of neck

Doo rags

Side ponytail

Infomercials proclaimed that peach fuzz could be made to look like "hair" with the aid of GPH Hair Formula. The product was a colored spray that would cover a small amount of hair and make it appear to be fuller. The end result after use was the look of having your head painted by vandals.

Hair Club for Men

Spiked/punk cut

The greasy look

Long sideburns

The flat top

The crew cut

Shaved head

Toupee

Bun

Mop

Pigtails

Permed look

The crop

The goatee

Fads

Fuzzy dice

New-age crystals

High-fiber diets

Buffalo nickels

Indian-head pennies

Furbies

Tickle Me Elmo

Virtual pets

Pet rocks

Hula hoop

Baby-on-board signs

Lava lamps

Rubik's cube

Lucky rabbit's foot

Cabbage Patch Kids

Pop rocks

Kewpie dolls

Garfield with suction-cup feet

Concocted in 1975 by a California advertising man named Gary Dahl, this utterly baffling, goofy idea blossomed into a nation-wide craze within a few short months and made its inventor a millionaire just as quickly.

Slap bracelet

Mood ring

Fuzzy neon-colored feet with adhesive backs

Moped

Goop

Ouija board

Slogan buttons

Super balls

Care Bears

Teenage Mutant Ninja Turtles

Trolls

Fads

Stupid bumper stickers

Koosa

Pogo stick

Hacky sack

Pogs

Chia pet

Virtual pet

Key fobs

Dance marathons

Flagpole sitting

Goldfish swallowing

Panty raids

Telephone booth stuffing

Streaking

Happy face signs

Pac Man

The peace symbol

Gak

Zodiac merchandise

Beanie Babies

Koosh balls

Friendship pins

Mosh pits, crowd surfing, stage diving

Giga pet

Expressions and language

"Play it again, Sam"

"Galoshes"

"Grammar school"

"Icebox"

"Yesterday's spilled milk"

"Keen"

"The bee's knees"

"The cat's pajamas"

Legendary fictional quote reportedly said by Rick (Humphrey Bogart) to piano player Sam in *Casablanca*. Too bad that the actual line is never said—rather, a drunken, lovetorn Bogey simply says, "Play it!"

Expressions and language

"The cat's meow"

"As if"

"...See a man about a horse"

"Nifty"

"Groovy"

"Cool beans"

"Powder my nose"

"Hot tomato"

"Kiss my grits"

"Grody to the max"

"Totally tubular"

"Swell"

"...See a man about a dog"

"In like Flynn"

"Word to your mother"

"Heyyy...!"

"Sit on it!"

"Whatever"

"Gnarly"

"Chickie," or any girl reference with an "-ie" suffix

"Rad"

"Radical"

34

"Dude"

"Boss"

"Let's do lunch"

"Daddy-O"

Mod

Flapper

Grease monkey

Getting in touch with your "inner child"

"I just wanted to touch base with you"

Gigolo

Jive

Filling station

Tin lizzie

Heavy metal

Cops and robbers

"Rock jock"

Punk

"Male chauvinist pig"

Surf and turf

Groupie

Acid rock

Flower child

Hard rock

Uptight

"Sock it to me"

Rumpus room

Bebop

The "flipside"

Yuppie

Preppie

"Don't have a cow, man!"

"Having a meltdown"

"Go ahead, make my day"

Yiddish

Ebonics

Esperanto

Pig latin

Names

Myron

Ernie

Bertha

Martha

Eugene

Virginia

Ruth

Gay

Marsha/Marcia

Matilda

Penelope

Eloise

Heloise

Harriet

Bernadette

Edgar

Melvin

Matilda, a name originating from the English, Norwegian, and Swedish languages means "battle maid" or "mighty in battle." Although it is definitely not gaining popularity, it still ranked 707th in names for females in the 1990 Census.

Florence

Skippy

Flip

Dirwood

Cassius Clay (now Muhammed Ali)

School

Dunce caps

Slide rules

Reform school

The "new" math

T-squares

40

Logarithmic tables

Writing in "script"

Social promotion

Chalk boards

Shelter drills

Old school annuals

Pencil case

Real lead pencils

Reinforcements

Book straps

Calculators not allowed in class

Those good old chalk boards, so prevalent in schools for decades, provided more than just a place for teachers (and kids) to scribble. Erasers made for handily tossed attention-grabbers, and many a detention hour was spent banging the choking dust out of them. However, said dust became a health issue, so the cleanliness of dry-erase markers and overhead projectors has made history of the squeaky writing utensils.

"School" shoes

Sock hops

Gymsuits

Metal lunch box

Thermos with TV characters

Half-day kindergarten

School hours from 9 a.m. to ...?

Penmanship

Basal readers

Forced busing

Affirmative action

"Instructional media centers" replacing libraries

Abacus

Prayer in public schools

Summer vacation

Grammar

The word "denigrate"

The word "shall"

The word "whom"

The words "all right"

"Towards" being replaced by "toward"

Agreement between pronoun and antecedent

Semicolons

The difference between the meanings of the words "might" and "may"

Restrictive and non-restrictive phrases and clauses using "that" and "which"

The complete sentence

Occupations

TV repairman

Stenographer

Phone/switchboard operator

Cigarette girl

Street peddler

Encyclopedia salesperson

Fuller Brush man

Tin man

Elevator operator

Toll taker

PBX operator

Organ grinder

Ragman

Knife sharpener

Ice man

World War II brought about automatic programming that was eventually applied to elevators and made room for one more in the lift, much to the chagrin of unemployed elevator operators.

Boat maker

Cotton picker

Shoeshine man

Keypunch operator

Air traffic controller

Home delivery man for food items

Bank teller

The Workplace

Hierarchical companies

Employee loyalty

Smoking at your desk

46

Reengineering

Empowerment

Sexual harassment

Male-dominated companies

Forced retirement at age 65

The 40-hour, 5-day workweek

Job security

Office stuff

Paperweight

Time clock in office setting

Hand-cranked Rolodex files

Manual typewriter

Electric typewriter

Typewriter ribbons

Carbon paper

The concept of typing two documents simultaneously may have been revolutionary in 1880. But with the invention of the photocopy machine in 1948, the idea of carbon paper was on its way to the shredder.

Correctype

5 1/2" floppy disks

Overhead projectors

Punch cards

Key punchers

Mimeograph machines

BASIC programming

Office stuff

Pocket protector for pens

Quill pen

Fountain pen with ink cartridges

Typewriter eraser ribbon

Typesetter

Telex

1999 calendar

Comebacks

Donald Trump

The bald eagle

Jane Pauly

Mr. Whipple

Twiggy

John Travolta

Continental Airlines

The buffalo

Marv Albert

Yesssssh! Marv's cross-dressing is not biting back at him (pun intended). Albert just signed a multiyear contract with NBC to cover the NBA, as well as boxing and hockey in the 2000 Olympics.

Comebacks

2001 2001

2001

People
in the
spotlight
(and out)

2001
2001
2001

Fifteen minutes of fame

Kenneth Starr

Paula Jones

Kathleen Willey

Bernhard Goetz

Linda Tripp

Billy Carter

Roger Clinton

Divine Brown

Kato the Dog

Donna Rice

Vigilante or defensive citizen? No matter how history ends up painting him, Goetz' actions have created controversial platforms on which issues such as personal liberties, gun control, and the proliferation of violence in our society remain endlessly debated.

54

Larena and John Wayne Bobbit

Gennifer Flowers

Michael Milkin

Oliver North

Kato Kaelin

Paula Barbieri

Mark Fuhrman

Chris Darden

Mary Beth Whitehead & Baby M

Louise Woodward

Amy Fisher

Joey Buttafuoco

Jean Harris

Anita Hill

Tonya Harding

Nancy Kerrigan

Judith Exner

Baby Jessica (fell into a well)

Richard Jewel (falsely accused
in Atlanta Olympics bombing)

Baby Louise Brown (first test-tube baby)

Amy Grossberg and Brian Peterson

Lesson one on how *not* to get ahead in the cutthroat world of professional figure skating: don't attempt to have your competition assassinated. In Tonya Harding's case, her failed attempt at doing an Oswald led to her own Bay of Pigs: worldwide abhorrence and a flatlined career both on and off the ice.

Fifteen minutes of fame

Couples

Donald and Ivana Trump

Demi Moore and Bruce Willis

Geri Hall and Mick Jagger

Jim Carry and Lauren Holly

Elizabeth Taylor and anyone

Michael Jackson and Lisa Marie Presley

Pamela Sue Anderson and Tommy Lee

Madonna and Sean Penn

Brooke Shields and Andre Agassi

Woody Allen and Mia Farrow

Rosanne Barr and Tom Arnold

Parker Stevenson and Kirstie Alley

Ralph Fiennes and Alex Kingston

Emilio Esteves and Paula Abdul

Halle Berry and David Justice

Linda Hamilton and James Cameron

Jerry Seinfeld and Shoshanna Lonstein

Farrah Fawcett and Ryan O'Neal

Jim and Tammy Faye Bakker

Dennis Rodman and Carmen Elektra

Burt Reynolds and Loni Anderson

Couples

58

Billy Joel and Christie Brinkley

Kenneth Branagh and Emma Thompson

Richard Gere and Cindy Crawford

Sarah Ferguson and Prince Andrew

Melanie Griffith and Don Johnson

The original Blues Brothers

Donald Trump and Marla Maples

And don't forget...

Luke and Laura *(General Hospital)*

Ross and Rachel *(Friends)*

Doug Ross and Carol Hathaway *(ER)*

Jerry (Seinfeld) and Elaine *(Benes)*

The Coneheads *(Saturday Night Live)*

Archie and Edith *(All in the Family)*

Mork and Mindy

Lois and Clark Kent *(Superman)*

Lois and Superman

Batman and Robin

J.R. and Sue Ellen Ewing *(Dallas)*

Bobby and Pamela Ewing *(Dallas)*

Gumby and Pokey

Rhett and Scarlett *(Gone with the Wind)*

Couples

People gone but not forgotten

JFK Jr.

Florence Joyner

Jerry Garcia

Tiny Tim

Arthur Godfrey

George Burns

Danny Kaye

Lucille Ball and Desi Arnaz

Fred Astaire

Gene Autry

People
gone but not forgotten

Roy Rogers

Jimmy Stewart

Frank Sinatra

Sonny Bono

Lloyd Bridges

James Cagney

Elvis

Princess Diana

Jessica Tandy

Colonel Sanders

Owen Hart

Linda McCartney

Joe DiMaggio

His records might eventually be broken, but the late and lamented "Yankee Clipper" will always be remembered as the elder statesman of baseball, a gentleman who inspired people both on and off the field.

Mother Theresa

World War I veterans

Dr. Seuss

Saturday Night Live
- Gilda Radner
- John Belushi
- John Candy
- Phil Hartman
- Chris Farley

The Gambino family under the rule of Gotti Sr.

Survivors of the *Titanic*

People forgotten but not gone

Tom Jones

Mr. T

Pam Grier

Tony Orlando

Englebert Humperdink

Perry Como

Robert Goulet

Art Linkletter

Petula Clark

Karen Valentine

People forgotten but not gone

Chad Everett

David Soul

Glen Campbell

Isaac Hayes

Chuck Barris

Charles Nelson Reilly

Mayim Bialik

Rodney Dangerfield

Shirley Temple

Pee Wee Herman

David Caruso

Don't typecast Charles Nelson Reilly! He isn't just a star of 1980s game shows such as *The Match Game* and *Hollywood Squares*. He was in many blockbuster movies such as *Babes in Toyland* (1997), *A Troll in Central Park* (1994), and everyone's perennial favorite, *Rock-A-Doodle* (1992).

People who will be around forever

Dick Clark

2001
2001

2001

Fun and games

2001
2001
2001

Amusements and entertainment

The song "1999" by Prince

Smellovision

3-D glasses

Cinerama

Atari 2600

Hundreds of games and tens of thousands of Atari consoles sold, and millions of kids of the 80s made the Atari 2600 game system a veritable legend. In hindsight, a game of Frogger is still more fun than any of the gross-out horror death games of the 1990s.

Drive-in movies

Drive-in restaurants

Sega video games

Nickelodeons

World fairs

70

Sean Connery as James Bond

A movie that costs less than $10

Family time, minus the TV

Susan Lucci without an Emmy

Single screen movie theaters

Yodeling

Discotheques

Pac Man

Player pianos

Playboy clubs

Playboy bunnies

Rocky 6

AfterM*A*S*H

Psychic hotlines

Muzak

The TV western

Commodore 64 video games

Movies at Radio City Music Hall

Jukeboxes

Big band music

Movie palaces with brightly lit marquees and names like "Rialto" and "Bijou"

Amusements and entertainment

Some of the great
original Broadway theaters

The company formerly known as
20th Century-Fox

Edibles and drinkables

Spam

Two-cent plain

Chocolate Babies

Ambrosia (jello, marshmallows, and fruit)

Salisbury steaks

Velveeta

Cheez Wiz

Maypo

Bosco

Cocoa Marsh

Yipes Its Stripes 5-flavor fruit gum

Flavor straws

Steak tartare

> Take uncooked beef. Stir in some *E. coli* bacteria. Contract food poisoning. Mmm mmm good.

Fluffernutter

Charlotte Russe

Fondue

Frito Lay lemonade

McLean Deluxe Burger (made with seaweed)

Ovaltine

Chiffon margarine

Funny Face drink mix

Jello mold salad

Fiddle Faddle

Cereal

Kaboom

King Vitamin

Freakies

Sugar Smacks

Booberry

Ghostbusters

Gremlins

Smurfberry Crunch

One of the great sugar-laden cereals of the 1980s. Berry goodness, mixed in with animated cartoon fun. However, once the Smurf craze went stale, so did the cereal.

Cabbage Patch

Candy

Marathon bars

Caravelle

Powerhouse bars

Candy cigarettes

Mary Janes

Reggie Bars

Edibles and drinkables

Laffy Taffy

Charleston Chew

Rally

Chunky

Wax lips

Dots

Jujubes

Pez

Good 'n Plenty/Choo Choo Charlie

Rock candy

Milk Duds

Edibles and drinkables

Lickamaid/Fun Dip

Candy necklaces

The waves of news stories concerning pin-possessed candies in the 1980s reduced our trust in unwrapped candy or candied apples.

Nonwrapped Halloween candy

Drinkables (alcoholic)

Fuzzy Navel

Tom Collins

Rheingold

Highball

Pink Squirrel

Alabama Slammer

Harvey Wallbanger

Billy Beer

Gimlet

Brass Monkey

Ballantine

Zima

It was "zomething different" at first, but the bubbly alcoholic beverage fizzled a few years after its introduction. Zo much for being different.

Boilermaker

Schlitz

Strohs

Rusty Nail

"Soda pop" culture

Coke cans with pull tabs

Coke with pry off caps

Coke 2

The "New" Coke

Crystal (clear) Pepsi

Pepsi Lite

The "Uncola" (made without "cola nuts")

Fresca

Tab

Coke machines with the long narrow doors

Toys

Metal Slinky

Skate keys

Soft vinyl baby toys

Roller skates

Roller skates gave us individual mobility, and freed us from machinery, until the advent of skateboards, the next evolutionary step. Now that Rollerblades have offset both, it looks like brand new pairs of roller skates and brand new keys are forever attic-bound

Metal pedal cars

Cast iron toys

Ouija boards

Real bamboo fishing poles

Bubble gum in packs of baseball cards

Wooden Lincoln Logs

Toys

Family bicycles

Silly Putty

Anything in genuine wood

Jacobs Ladder

Teddy Ruxpin

Wacky Packages

Toy ball

Big Wheels

Sea Monkeys

Spirographs

Gnip Gnop

Rock 'Em Sock 'Em Robots

Barrel of Monkeys

Stratego

Sit & Spin

Garbage Pail Kids stickers

Demolition Derby

Shrinky Dinks

My Little Pony

Lite Brite

Pound Puppies and Pound Purries

Care Bears

Toys

Wuzzles

Lawn darts

Garfield stuff

Snoopy Sno-cone machine

Pull toys with wooden pull handles

Easy Bake oven

Silly String

Ring-A-Ding

Zany Zappers

Stickers of all kinds

Simon

Original Weebles

Fisher Price little wooden people

Smurfs

Magic 8-ball

The Magic 8-ball knows your fortune. Sort of. Like any magic trick, there is always a simple method to its madness—this one involves blue liquid and an icosahedral with various "yes", "no", and "answer unclear, try again later" statements.

Giant Lego

Whirligig

Scooter

Pogo stick

Cap gun

Flexible Flyer real wood sled

Hopscotch

Hess toy truck

ViewMaster

Dolls and action figures

Dressy Bessy & Dapper Dan

Strawberry Shortcake

Holly Hobbie

Jody, an Old Fashion Girl

The Sunshine Family

Tuesday Taylor

Chrissy, Velvet, Mia

Sweet April

Tiny Tears

Chatty Cathy

Cabbage Patch Kids

Six Million Dollar Man & Bionic Woman

Mr. T.

Aunt Jemima

Tron

Transformers

Stretch Armstrong

Evel Kenievel

1984 brought on the battle between the peaceful Autobots and the evil Decepticons. Young boys all over the United States enhanced their dexterity by manipulating these toys from machinery to robots.

Monchichi

Hello Kitty

Voltron

HeMan

Snorks

California Raisins

Little Kiddle

Flatsy

Betsy Wetsy

Chatty Patty

Baby Skates

Toys

Crayon colors

Indian Red

Flesh

Raw Umber

Lemon Yellow

Crayon colors

Maize

Green Blue

Orange Red

Orange Yellow

Violet Blue

A lot has changed since 1903 when the first Crayola crayons were sold for a nickel. Colors have changed due to outdated events (Prussian Blue) and ethnic awakening (Indian Red and Flesh). However, kids remain the same; the top colors of the 90s are still the old stand-by: red and blue.

Blue Gray

Prussian Blue

Books

OJ's *I Want To Tell You*

Valley of the Dolls

I'm OK, You're OK

The Pentagon Papers

It Takes a Village

The Feminine Mystique

The Preppy Handbook

Future Shock

90

Beanie Baby Handbook

How to Live With a Cubaholic

Monica's Story

Real Men Don't Eat Quiche

The Scarsdale Diet

The Starr Report

1984

The Greening of America

101 Uses for A Dead Cube

Been working on your Rubik's cube since 1985? Perhaps it's time to give up and find yourself a copy of this brilliant piece of modernist American literature.

50 Urgent Things You Need to Do Before the Millennium

Anything by Harold Robbins, Jacqueline Susanne, or Jackie Collins

TV shows (Career Press favorites)

Cheers

M*A*S*H

The Magic Garden

Moonlighting

Dr. Who

Warner Bros. cartoons

Falcon Crest

The Jeffersons

Fantasy Island

Happy Days

Seinfeld

Welcome Back, Kotter

Donna Reed

Green Acres

All in the Family

Murphy Brown

Home Improvement

Coach

Knight Rider

The greatest comedy in the history of television and the quintessential sitcom. For a show seemingly about nothing, its multitude of somethings ingeniously reflected the air of pre-millennium tensions and social schemes that make us so complicatedly human. It will never be eclipsed, and will always be missed. And that's a shame.

Star Trek (original and new series)

The Dukes of Hazzard

The Golden Girls

Mad About You

I Love Lucy

Twin Peaks

Homicide: Life on the Street

The Outer Limits (original)

Taxi

Barney Miller

The Bob Newhart Show

Our Miss Brooks

My Favorite Martian

Lassie

The Mickey Mouse Club (original)

Cosby

Your Show of Shows

The Ed Sullivan Show

The Honeymooners

Family Ties

Little House on the Prairie

Dynasty

The Paper Chase

Dallas

St. Elsewhere

Leave It to Beaver

Another World

Hill Street Blues

The Muppet Show

And now for something completely different...Perhaps one of the most brilliant TV shows of all time, the *Flying Circus* transformed parrots, full frontal nudity, lumberjacks, and confused cats into side-splitting skits. The show aired from 1969 to 1974, although it rivals most comedies on the tube today.

Monty Python's Flying Circus

Mary Tyler Moore

American Bandstand

Rhoda

Eight is Enough

Sisters

The Flip Wilson Show

Mr. Ed

Queen For a Day

Remington Steele

The Nanny

Scarecrow and Mrs. King

Quincy

The Twilight Zone

Kid TV

Wonderama

New Zoo Revue

Romper Room

HR Puff 'n' stuff

Barney

Magilla Gorilla

Pinky Lee

Clarabelle

Mr. Greenjeans

Lamb Chop

The Peanut Gallery

Charlie McCarthy

Kermit

Howdy Doody

"What time is it? It's Howdy Doody Time!" *USA Today* listed Howdy Doody as the number two show in "TV Shows that Shaped Our Lives" (June 19, 1997). Contrary to today's TV fare of sex and violence, the influence was positive.

Mr. Hooper

Kukla, Fran, & Ollie

Krazy Kat

Captain Kangaroo

Jerry Mahoney & Knucklehead Smiff

Princess SummerFallWinterSpring

Talk show hosts

Arsenio Hall

Phil Donahue

Steve Allen

Greg Kinnear

Carney Wilson

Magic Johnson

Merv Griffin

Pat Sajak

Jack Paar

Geraldo Rivera

In 1989, a new concept in TV talk was launched on the CBS Network. In 1989, it was also laid to rest. Pat Sajak, who has hosted *Wheel of Fortune* since 1981, tried to capture viewers with lively conversation. It wasn't lively enough.

100

Chevy Chase

David Frost

David Susskind

Joey Bishop

Mike Douglas

Dick Cavett

Tom Snyder

The Tonight Show starring Johnny Carson

Shows we're glad will make it

Frasier

ER

SportsCenter

The Practice

Law and Order

60 Minutes

Sesame Street

The X-Files

Sports

Steffi Graf

Brooklyn Dodgers

Washington Senators

St. Louis Browns

Jai alai

Croquet

Handball

Tetherball

Designated hitter rule

Pitchers in the American league breathed a sigh of relief when Ron Blomberg stepped up to the plate on April 6, 1973, as the first official designated hitter. Now free from the burden of hitting, pitchers could pursue other interests such as spitting, chewing tobacco, scratching, dugout tantrums…

Shuffleboard

Horseshoe throwing

Wiffleball

Patrick Ewing's knees

Oakland Raiders

Dodge ball

Michael Jordan, baseball player

Garth Brooks, baseball player

Dennis Rodman

Pete Rose's Hall of Fame nomination

1998 Olympic basketball all-star team

Stickball

Secretariat

Cheap seats at any major league ballpark

Wooden golf drivers (aka "woods")

Yankee Stadium

Tiger Stadium

Sports

Fenway Park

King Dome

Officiating by replay

The doubleheader

Music groups

Led Zeppelin

The Partridge Family

ABBA

Milli Vanilli

KC and the Sunshine Band

The undisputed kings of disco, KC and the boys have enjoyed a rebirth (of sorts) in the 90s thanks to the likes of Mike Myers in his *Austin Powers* guise and Miller Beers use of "Get Down Tonight" on their TV commercials. Shake, shake, shake...

The 1990s Backstreet Collective (Backstreet Boys, 98°, N*Sync, et al.)

The New Kids on the Block

Rick Springfield

Paul Revere and the Raiders

Menudo

Country Joe and the Fish

The Bee Gees

Air Supply

The Spice Girls

Iron Butterfly

Duran Duran

Bananarama

The Village People

Kajagoogoo

A-ha

Asia

Boston

The Knack

Survivor

Men without Hats

The entire genre known as "progressive rock"

Spandau Ballet

Blind Faith

Corey Hart

Toto

Men at Work

The Outfield

Dances

Stroll

Locomotion

Lindy

Jitterbug

Music groups

Mashed Potato

Chicken dance

Break dancing

Slam dancing

Electric slide

Hustle

Disco

Limbo

Swing

Moonwalk

Line dancing

Oh please, please, please may this dance go the way of the dodo. Introduced in the 80s, the electric slide is a staple of many a wedding, banquet, barbecue, or social, and it is reported to be "fun." Hopefully, it will end in the up-and-coming century, but such evil is not easily conquered.

Dances

Watusi

Pony

Twist

Frug

Macarena

Swim

Jerk

Monster Mash

Walk

Shimmy

Pop culture

Fear of Y2K

Hashish

Woodstock

Peace, love, good tunes…and don't forget the mud! The 1969 festival was the greatest music event of all time…with all the sanitary problems you would get with 300,000 people crammed onto a field. The "Woodstocks" of the 90s, however, have become huge commercial monstrosities.

Hippies

Disco music

Malt shops

Teenage Mutant Ninja Turtles

New York City movie ticket under $10

High school sock hops

Independent bookstores

Breakdancing

The art of yodeling

Black and white TVs

Peace buttons

Go-go boots

Reel-to-reel tape recorders

Batman mania in the 60s

A generation that has not lived with the AIDS epidemic

Slide rules

Draft cards

Pop culture

Speed bikes

Banana seats

Burma Shave road signs

Barney

He may love you, he may love me, but most people don't love him back. The annoying purple dinosaur emerged in 1988 to the joyful squeals of children…and the pathetic screams of adults. Don't believe us? Check out yahoo.com. As of this writing, there are 19 anti-Barney sites…and only 7 pro-Barney sites.

Art deco

Andy Warhol

Wolfman Jack

Mel's diner

Pop art

Campbell's Soup garbage can

Wish lists of things that shouldn't make it to the next century

Archie comics

Communes

The lunch counter at Woolworth's

Drive-in diners and car hops

Double features at the movies

This book

Pop culture

2001 2001

2001

Ad slogans and the art of the jingle

2001 2001

2001

Ad slogans and jingles

How many of these can you guess?
(answers start on page 125)

1. Plop, plop, fizz, fizz,
   oh what a relief it is!

2. It's the *slow* ketchup

3. You can trust your car to the men
   who wear the star

4. The quicker picker-upper

5. When you care enough to
   send the very best

6. Good to the last drop

7. The Uncola

8. A little dab'll do ya

9. Mmm mm good

10. You're soaking in it now!

11. Double your pleasure, double your fun

12. Reach out and touch someone

13. Look how good you look now!

14. We bring good things to life

15. With nooks and crannies to hold the butter

16. Melts in your mouth, not in your hands

17. Can't pinch an inch!

18. Ho, ho, ho!

19. We'll leave a light on for you

20. Bring out the best!

21. When it rains, it pours

22. The great American chocolate bar

23. You deserve a break today

24. We do chicken right!

25. Look Ma, no cavities!

26. Mikey likes it—he hates everything!

27. Something special in the air

28. Snap! Crackle! Pop!

29. Don't leave home without it!

Ad slogans and jingles

30. I'm the loneliest guy in town

31. Just for the taste of it!

32. Its ¼ cleansing cream

33. Breakfast of champions

34. Fast, fast, fast relief

35. Have it *your* way!

36. Does she...or doesn't she?
    Only her hairdresser knows for sure.

37. Diamonds are forever

38. I'd rather fight than switch!

39. 99 and 44/100% pure

40. I'd like to teach the world
    to sing in perfect harmony

41. Ring around the collar

42. Takes a licking and keeps on ticking

43. Where's the beef?

44. Beer that made Milwaukee famous

45. 2 scoops of raisins in every box

46. Leave the driving to us

47. You'll wonder where the yellow went

48. Let your fingers do the walking

49. Always a bridesmaid, but never a bride

50. Bet you can't eat just one!

Ad slogans and jingles

122

...And can you fill in these blanks?
(answers start on page 129)

1. Pardon me, do you have some ___?

2. Aren't you glad you use ___? Don't you wish everybody did?

3. Fall into the ___!

4. Bert & Harry ___

5. Have you driven a ___ lately?

6. ___ tastes good like a cigarette should

7. When you've said ___, you've said it all!

8. Fly the friendly skies of _____

9. Uh-oh ___

10. The best part of waking up is ____ in your cup

11. Know what comes between me and my ____? Nothing!

12. Wouldn't you really rather have a ____ this year?

13. Leggo my ____

14. I'd walk a mile for a ____

15. There's more for your life at ____

16. Let ____ put you in the driver's seat

17. I dreamed I went shopping in my ____ bra

18. I want to be a _____ kid!

19. Wow! I could have had a __!

Ad slogans and jingles

...And who could forget?

Joe Camel

The cigarette-smokin' cartoon character that hocked cigarettes in the 80s and 90s has been sent packing back to the desert. Concerned parents' groups complained that Joe made kids want to smoke. R. J. Reynolds relented, giving Joe his pink slip.

Smokey the Bear

The Pillsbury Doughboy

Morris the Cat

Buster Brown and Tide

The Procter & Gamble logo

Giant cigarette billboards

Cigarette ads on TV and in magazines

Mr. Coffee commercials with Joe DiMaggio

Bob Dole's ads for erectile dysfunction

Answers:

1. Alka Seltzer

2. Heinz

3. Texaco

4. Bounty

5. Hallmark

6. Maxwell House

7. 7-Up

8. Brylcreem

9. Campbell's Soup

10. Palmolive liquid

11. Wrigley's Doublemint gum

12. AT&T

13. Avon

14. General Electric

15. Thomas's English muffins

16. M&M's

17. Special K cereal

18. Green Giant

19. Motel 6

20. Hellmann's

Ad slogans and jingles

21. Morton Salt

22. Hershey's

23. McDonald's

24. Kentucky Fried Chicken

25. Crest toothpaste

26. Life Cereal

27. American Airlines

28. Rice Krispies

29. American Express

30. Maytag

31. Diet Coke

32. Dove soap

33. Wheaties

34. Anacin

35. Burger King

36. Clairol

37. DeBeers

38. Tarryton cigarettes

39. Ivory Soap

40. Coca Cola

41. Wisk detergent

42. Timex

43. Wendy's

44. Schlitz

45. Post Raisin Bran

46. Greyhound

47. Pepsodent

48. Yellow Pages

49. Listerine

50. Lay's potato chips

Fill-ins:

1. Grey Poupon

2. Dial soap

Ad slogans and jingles

14. Camel

15. Sears

16. Hertz

17. Maidenform

18. Toys 'R' Us

19. V-8

2001
2001
2001

Things that have made. life easier

2001
2001
2001

Electronics

TVs without remote controls

Beta tapes and machines

Analog clocks

Instamatic cameras

Black and white TVs

Flash cubes

TVs with picture tubes

Hi-fidelity systems

TVs with knobs or dials

8mm movie projectors and cameras

136

16mm movie projectors and cameras

Slide projectors

8-track tapes and players

Kodak disk camera

Cameras that takes 126-size film

8-track adapters for the car

The 78 rpm record

The 45 rpm record

The 33 rpm record

Record players for 45s (singles)

2-head VCRs

UHF

Phonograph needles

Transistor radios

Polaroid Swinger camera

Rabbit ears (TV antennae)

Electric knife sharpener

Radio tubes

Radio tube tester

Electric fuses

Adding machine

Rotary dial telephone

Electronics

Princess phone

Cassette player

Brownie camera

The Rabbit

The Odyssey² computer game system

Pong consoles

Intellevision

Colecovision

Filmstrip projectors with separate cassette players

X-ray machines in shoe stores (used to size shoes)

Dictaphone

Cassette answering machines

Gramophone

Reel-to-reel tape recorder

Megaphone

Victrola

Walkie-talkie

Manual typewriter

Apple's Newton electronic personal assistant

Strobe lights

Cigarette vending machines

Electronics

Mechanical switchboard

Sony Watchman

DIVX

Technology

The *Challenger*

Dolly, the cloned sheep

Telephone party lines

Windmills

The Y2K bug and Y2K compliance

"Born" in July 1996 at the Roslin Institute near Edinburgh, Scotland, Dolly was the first mammal to be cloned from a different sheep's cell. Named after singer Dolly Parton, Dolly has not only enjoyed a healthy existence, she has also given birth twice—the old-fashioned way. "Baby boomer" might soon take on a whole new meaning.

Fossil fuels

2x CD-ROM players

286 PCs

86 PCs

Wang computers

Rocket scientists

Batteries

Hydraulic elevators

IBM's PC Junior

Apple's original classic "Mac"

Microfiche

Technology

Wang cathode-ray tube word processors

Used up area codes

800 numbers

Microphones with wires

Telephones with wires

Household items

Genuine wooden furniture

Washboards

Heating systems that run on coal

Refrigerators that are not frost-free

Foam toilet seats (and covers)

Freon air conditioning

Suntan oil

Mercury thermometers

If you have an old mercury thermometer, beware! Mercury contamination can cause memory loss, emotional problems, fatigue, tremors, and extensive damage to the central nervous system.

Humidor

Spitoon

Clotheslines

Clothespins

Plastic slipcovers

Velvet curtains

Ceiling light pull chains

Cast iron bottle openers

144

Maytag wringer washer

Pedal driven sewing machines

Bean bag chairs

Philco radios

Inflatable furniture

Gas chandeliers

Cuckoo clock

Grandfather clock

Carpet beaters

Egg chair

Press-on-nails

Kerosene heater

Franklin stove

Irons that you heat on the stove

Oil lamp

High-flush toilet

Push lawn mowers

Shag carpeting

Bamboo doorway beads

Bottle caps lined with cork

Stove-top percolator

Wooden matches

Household items

146

Metal hotel keys

L'eggs "egg" containers

Macrame wall hangings

Tooth powder

Sun reflector

Fallout shelter

Zippo lighter

Hurricane lamp

Credenza

Vanity mirror tray with matching comb and brush set

A direct by-product of rampant 50s Communist paranoia, these constructs of the atomic age nearly became backyard staples throughout America. Though now an architectural relic, many government and older civilian buildings still sport the cinderblock, 'radiation-proof' anterooms.

Easy chair

Venetian blinds

Real talcum powder

Kitchen wares

Glass milk bottles

Crock pot

Fry Daddies and Fry Babies

Sandwich makers

Doughnut machine

Seal-a-Meal

Bottle opener for pry-off caps

Popcorn poppers

Electric knives

Ginsu knives

Jello molds

Crepe machine

Bread box

Cookie jar

Waxed paper

Welch's jelly jars

Fondue makers

Rotary egg beater

Avocado green kitchen appliances

Harvest gold kitchen appliances

Iceboxes

Formica top table and handleback dinette chairs

Home canning

Merry Mushroom kitchen accessories

Malted machine

Hard-boiled egg slicers

Medicine and health

Little black bag

Phen-Phen

Polio and the polio vaccine

House calls

Pills in capsule form

Sharing hypodermic needles

Mustard plaster

Camphorated oil

Castor oil

Guggle-muggle

Raw materials for medicines

Midwives

Smallpox and the smallpox vaccine

The Dalkon Shield

Laetrile

Iron lung

Insulin

Silicon breast implants

Swine-flu vaccine

Radium cures

Non-tamper resistant medicine bottles

It all started in 1964 with the first pair of implants. By 1995, according to the FDA, there were approximately one million women with implants. Problems with leaky silicon implants lead to the creation of saline implants.

Folk medicine

Herbal medicine

Bubonic plague

Syphilis

Measles

Chicken pox

Pellagra

Mercury dental fillings

Silver and gold dental fillings

Mad cow disease

E-coli

Thalidomide

Botox injections to get rid of wrinkles

HMOs

Transportation

The Yugo

Family bicycles

Tiger tails on bicycles

Schwinn Sting-Ray

Station wagons

Banana bike seat

Cars without power steering

Dodge Dart

Mopeds

Car fins

Rambler

The DeLorean

The DeLorean conquered time travel in the hit movie *Back to the Future*, but the "ethical" car did not manage to conquer the car market, as only 8,600 were manufactured from 1981 to 1983.

Gremlin

Pacer

Big-fendered bicycle

Corvair

Bench front seats

Rumble seats

Pinto

Wind screens

Metal baskets on bicycles

Plugs and points

Leaded gas

The Edsel

K-cars

Trans Am

VW Vans

CB radios in "civilian" cars

Wide-seat bicycle

Transportation

Rear-facing car seats

LTD

Wire wheels

White-wall tires

Full meal served on airplanes

Duster

Mini license plates on bicycles

Free deck of cards on airplanes

Checker cab

Bicycle bells

Spark plugs

Rivets

Steam locomotives

HOV lanes

Catalytic converters

Fuzzy dice

Diesel cars

Wheelbarrow

Covered bridges

Cobblestone roads

Cars with driver-side only
rearview mirrors

Transportation

158

Suburban wagon

Biplane

Model T

Ice truck

The Autoskate

Drag racing on the street

Hood ornaments

Finned rear fenders

Manual windows on cars

Snow chains

Snow tires

Propeller plane

Rear-wheel drive

Jalopy

Vent windows on cars

Rumble seats

Speed bike

The Starship *Enterprise*

Airlines

Eastern

Pan American World

160

Frontier

Ozark

Braniff

Piedmont

Republic

Western

AirCal

ValuJet

Building materials

Log cabins

Fiberglass insulation

Brick

Lead-based paint

Plaster walls

Blown-in foam insulation

Aluminum siding

Copper wiring

Lead pipes

Asbestos

Cinderblock foundations

Cinderblock house foundations are notorious for flooding, as the concrete begins to decompose. In addition to flooded basements, cinderblock foundations also leak harmful radon gas, a problem many in the Northeast face. The future is firm…in firm poured concrete foundations.

Building materials

2001
2001
2001

The world at large

2001 2001

2001

Stores and businesses

Five and ten stores

Woolworth's

Quackenbush

Alexanders

Orbachs

General stores

Penny candy store

Luncheonette with soda fountain

Malt shops

Korvette's

It's a superstore world. The age of the mom-and-pop shop, the corner specialty store that was a neighborhood icon spanning generations, has gone the way of the dinosaur, replaced by airplane hangar-sized behemoths with affordable prices and a tonnage of inventory. A trend for the better, or a trend for the worse?

Franklin Simon

Caldor

J Peterman

Fix-it shops

Mall video arcades

Finast

Bohacks

Newberry's

A&S

Mays

Bambergers

Gimbels

Wanamakers

Butcher shop

Independent pharmacy

Bell Telephone stores

Horn & Hardart Automat

Nedicks

Ice cream parlor

Haberdashery

Sweatshops

The Soup Nazis soup stand

Environment

Clean air

Ozone layer

DDT

Agent Orange

Clean water

Landfills

Coral reefs

Coral reefs are currently home to more than percent of all marine life. As time goes on, we continue to kill them off with pollution, waste, and oil spills. It's time that we all chip in and start taking a closer look at how our lifestyles affect our environment.

Trees

Rainforests

Forests in the Pacific Northwest

Endangered species

Whooping crane

Bengal tiger

Northern spotted owl

Crocodile

Cheetah

Black rhinoceros

Giant panda

Dodo bird

California condor

170

Politics and the world scene

Monica Mania

Income tax-free states

German reunification

Various European currencies

Social Security

Welfare

Abortion clinics

Illegal marijuana

U.S. involvement in the Panama Canal

The Cold War

Communism

The Berlin Wall

MIR space station

The Iron Curtain

Skylab

Watergate

Blacklisting

> In 1947, the "red scare" terrified the nation. Senator Joseph McCarthy focused his hunt for "reds" on Hollywood. When the dust finally cleared in 1954, over 300 people were blacklisted in the Hollywood community, among them Lillian Hellman, Dashiell Hammett, Bertolt Brecht, and Ring Lardner Jr.

Whitewater

Détente

The Ugandan Space Program

The Independent Counsel statute

Politics and the world scene

172

Irangate

Sputnik

Apartheid

Countries

East Germany

USSR

Gorbachev's glasnost and perestroika brought about freedom and openness in a formally oppressive nation. However, the Russians and other member states of the former Soviet Union now have poverty, pollution, and increased corruption to deal with.

Czechoslovakia

Yugoslavia

Zanzibar (now Madagascar/Tanzania)

Rhodesia (now Zimbabwe)

Zaire (Democratic Republic of the Congo)

Hong Kong as a British Colony

Concepts

Checks pre-printed 19__

The glass ceiling

The pink ghetto

One-hour photos

The endless hype about "the new millennium"

The $5 movie

All sense of decorum

174

Barrier-free access to the White House

The 10-cent phone call

Gospel singings

Tent revivals

Kids going door to door to raise money

Pay toilets

Emergency breakthrough phone calls

Bomb shelters

Foot stomping of grapes

Holding wakes in the home

Chivalry

Hitchhiking

Pamela Sue Anderson's bust

Women don't ask men out

Drink and drown bar nights

The paperless office

Fraternity hazing

Alcohol in fraternity houses

Smoking in public places

Dwindling AARP membership

Roseanne (Barr) as a singer

Bill Clinton as a politician

If Pamela doesn't want her implants, she needn't fear that they will go to waste. "Ripley's Believe it or Not Museum" in Hollywood wants them for an exhibit on beauty. Believe it...or not.

Concepts

176

Rent control

The single-paycheck family

Large families

Strip malls

Paying cash for anything

Paper money

The U.S. metric campaign

The "valley" girl

Full-service gas stations

Free maps at gas stations

Free gifts from gas stations

Free gifts from banks

Driver's licenses without pictures

"The customer is always right"

Home-cooked meals

Beatlemania

Real silver dollars

Susan B. Anthony dollar

S&H Green Stamps

Blue Chip stamps

Plaid stamps

Stamps that you lick

Introduced in 1979 to celebrate the legendary women's rights advocate, the coin failed in usage, as it looked too much like the Washington quarter. However, a new dollar coin featuring the famous Lewis and Clark's guide, Sacajawea, will be minted in 2000.

Concepts

178

The 4-cent stamp

Card catalogs in the library

Pennies

Personalized service

Silver certificates

The $2 bill

Separate men's and women's bathrooms

The nuclear family

Leaving doors unlocked

Telegrams

The "singing" telegram

Tourism in Uganda

Entering any government building without going through a metal detector

The blue plate special

Roadside diners

Mood lighting

Burning incense

Matchbooks in restaurants

Family farm

Shave and a haircut...2 bits!

The Borscht Belt

Concepts

Churches with unlocked doors

Mom-and-pop motels

Main Street, USA

Roadway etiquette

The American waistline

Living rooms

Rent control

Family dinner conversations

Meetings uninterrupted by the ring of somebody's beeper or cell phone

According to the AAA Foundation for Traffic Safety, violent incidents on the road have increased 51 percent from 1990 to 1996. Those statistics keep growing as more people on the road means more traffic, which means more frustration, which can mean more violence.

Institutions

KGB

Healthcare

Hare Krishnas

The East German Stazie (secret police)

Social Security

Medicare

Welfare

National Endowment for the Arts

Jim Jones and the People's Temple

David Koresh and the Branch Davidians

Marshall Applewhite and Heaven's Gate

New Year's Eve ball dropping in
Times Square

Buckingham Palace as the
Royal Family residence

Ballclubs that remain in their original town

Only two formalized political parties
in the U.S.

Communism

Newspapers, magazines, books, and
anything else that needs to be printed
on natural paper products

Sanitariums

College fraternities

Places

The Leaning Tower of Pisa

Washington's FBI Building tours

EuroDisney

Adult theaters in Times Square

Hong Kong as a British colony

Amusement parks (now theme parks)

The Panama Canal as a U.S. zone

Idlewild Airport (now JFK)

Chernobyl

Alcatraz

2001
2001

2001

Pre-millennium wish list

2001 2001

2001

Things we wish would still be around

The innocence of childhood

Independent bookstores

Home milk delivery

Street peddlers

Free playtime for kids

"Calling for" your friends

High interest rates on CDs

Bliss

Wish list

Things we're glad will make it

Gentrification

Environmental awareness

Newspaper ink that does not come off on your hands

Recycling

> Recycling became a social revolution for the masses in the 1980s. The jump in the percentage of recycled goods was most drastic between the late 80s and the early 90s. Projections into the 21st century show only upward movement.

Wonderbra

Books

Things we wish wouldn't make it

Computer viruses

Mike Tyson's career

Michael Jackson's recording career

Chain mail

Barney

Here's some good news and some bad news. Good news: There is no such thing as the "good times" e-mail virus. Bad news: Bill Gates isn't going to give you a Disney vacation. Why are you even reading these? Aren't you supposed to be working?

Wish list

Things we're glad won't make it

Segregation

Prohibition

Ishtar

Alan Dershowitz's mustache

Hitler, Stalin, Mussolini, et al.

Non-remote control home entertainment equipment

Corporal punishment in school

One of the worst comedies ever written. However, HBO, in its sadistic glory, seems to play this hunk of cinematic embarrassment every evening. One must wonder what Warren Beatty and Dustin Hoffman were thinking when they were looking at this script. Never has the talent of two great actors been squandered so badly. We all hope HBO loses the bloody tape someday.

Things that will be around forever

Century 21 Realtors

The song "21st Century Schizoid Man"
by King Crimson

Repairing the damage caused
by the Y2K bug

All the TV mini-series, movies of the
week, and investigatlve TV reports
about the many religious zealots,
reactionaries, cultists, New Agers, and
plain nutcases who offed themselves at
the stroke of midnight on January 1st,
2000 because they were convinced it
was the end of the world

Wish list